Reflections
on the
Savior

A Collection of Inspirational Poems to
Bring You Closer to Christ

Anna,

I hope these poems bring you peace,
to know that God loves every piece of
your heart. Keep talking with Him. Good
luck with the piano & violin!
— Kat Sanders

KATERINA SANDERS

ISBN 978-1-64003-042-8 (Paperback)
ISBN 978-1-64003-043-5 (Digital)

Copyright © 2017 Katerina Sanders
All rights reserved
First Edition

All rights reserved. No part of this publication may be reproduced, distributed, or transmitted in any form or by any means, including photocopying, recording, or other electronic or mechanical methods without the prior written permission of the publisher. For permission requests, solicit the publisher via the address below.

Covenant Books, Inc.
11661 Hwy 707
Murrells Inlet, SC 29576
www.covenantbooks.com

Contents

He Is the One 5
Choose Grace 6
Hope of God's Love 7
I Know My Savior 8
I Will Follow Thee 9
Forward in Faith 10
For Us All 12
Why He Sacrificed 13
Transform 14
Our Savior 15
He Gives Me Hope 16
This Life 17
You Are Never Alone 18
In Our Place 21
When He Comes Again 22
I'm on His Side 24
We Are Meant to Grow 25
Strength of Christ 26
Be Still 28
I'm Enough 30
He Loves Completely 32
He Chose Us 34
We Choose Him 35
Believe 36
The Best Gift 38

Saving Grace 39
He Draws Near unto Me 40
Will I Be There 42
Act in Faith 43
He Teaches Grace 44
His Peace 46
Choose Happiness 48
Trust 49
Grace 50
To Trust Is to Live 52
In My Life 54
Rise 56

He Is the One

He who walked on water
Walks with us hand in hand.
He who is the son of God
Came to save us sons of men.
He who radiates glorious light
Is the reason we choose to shine
He who knows our greatest worth
Gave His life so we
Could be divine.

He is perfect in strength
Follows only the Father.
He is perfect in will
Endures, does not falter.
He walks, He came,
He is, He gave
He follows, He endures,
He is the one.

Choose Grace

They mocked Him and they scorned Him,
They spat upon His face.
They cursed Him and they beat Him.
He treated them with grace.
Though despised and rejected
He never looked down.
He knew they lacked power over Him
Even when, with thorns, He was crowned.

They were filled with hate and anger,
Christ was filled with love.
They chose the devil as their master
Yet Christ followed God above.
The example that He sets for us
Is one of gentle grace,
To behold an enemy and instead of hate,
See only thy brother's face.

When striving to be something more
We call upon the Lord,
Our hearts being full with real intent,
He gives us support.
So, when others come and cause a scene
Don't look with hate upon their face.
Respond as Christ our example would,
And choose to act in grace.

Hope of God's Love

The transforming power of God
Rising the brightness from night.
All darkness cast out by
The brilliance of light!
Fear is replaced by the hope of God's love
Angels descend from our Father above.

We won't be alone in this journey we travel,
Our Father has given us friends
To buoy our courage and build up our faith
That we may endure to the end.

Oft times we find
We have fallen to our knees
But our Savior helps us to rise.
Through falling and rising
We find our strength increase
With a renewed hope in our eyes.

Yes, try then, keep trying,
Let weary hearts believe
Through the hope of God's love
We indeed find relief.

I Know My Savior

I know my Savior loves me.
I know He loves this world.
I know my Savior loves us,
Yes, every boy and girl.

I know that He protects us.
I know He shields our life.
I know that pain and heartache
Can be softened by His light.

I know of my Savior's power,
He heals me of my sins!
His atonement gives a blank slate
For me to try again.

I know my Savior has a plan,
I know He wants us home.
I know that we can make it
If we walk the path He has shown.

Through life, I have found healing.
Through trials, I know Christ is there.
Through repentance, I've found strength.
Through faith, I know my savior.

I Will Follow Thee

I said, "How can it be that He
Would go and suffer there for me?"
Christ said, "How could I not be
Your Savior, saving you from agony?"
God said, "How could I stand to keep my son
Knowing through Him all could be free?"
So how can I show my gratitude
And say, "I will follow thee."

His sacrifice, a weighty price,
A gift so freely given.
We promise to remember Him
And forsake all our sin,
To mourn with mourners, comfort others
And be a follower of Him.
We promise fully, with open heart
To help others return to Heaven.

Greatest happiness and joy
Is right around the bend.
As we devote our time and love
In the work of our Heavenly friend.
"Well done," He says, "thou hast been good, oh
Faithful servant of mine"
Come labor with me and here partake
Of Heaven's blessings divine

Forward in Faith

We don't have to understand it
For it to be right.
Through our mortal eyes
We have a fraction of God's sight.
But if we follow God's will
And refuse to fight,
Then we can partake
Of His uplifting light.

When we turn down a path,
Walk where we should not go;
Being influenced by the world,
Feeling tossed to and fro,
If we turn to God and ask
For His guidance here below,
Then from our fervent knocking,
The answers we shall know.

From our seeking and searching,
Pleading for a sign,
Heavenly Father lights the way,
The first step seems to shine.
Or maybe we just see
A small simple line
Marking faith moving forward,
Or doubt staying behind.

I take a deep breath,
Are our wills still aligned?
I've just got to go,
Now is the time.
He's given me the gear
To make it up this climb.
We'll take my first step together,
I've made up my mind.

Do I need the whole path
Laid out plainly? No.
Being led to act in faith
Made my testimony grow.
When I humble myself,
Let my pride come down low,
I find with God at the reel
I like watching His show.

When the morning comes,
Dawn breaking through night,
I find that with God
I've reached fantastic heights.
The sun overhead
On the clouds of pure white
I hear His calm voice
Saying my future is bright.

For Us All

Christ allowed Himself to be led
As a lamb, to be sacrificed for us.
Showing forth His infinite mercy,
He will stand between us and justice.
We had such a great price to pay,
With nowhere to turn, nowhere to run.
He conquered death, our sin, and our debt
Through His redeeming blood.

Now, which of us can redeem this love?
For whom was our Savior sent?
His blood was spilt for each of us;
To be saved we must repent.
Born again through Jesus Christ,
To become like Him we plead.
When converted and choosing to follow Him,
We become the Savior's seed.

He shows us mercy for He's felt our pain.
He knows our thoughts, He holds our heart,
He would do it, all for us all, again.

Why He Sacrificed

How wonderful, how splendid
Our Savior's sacrifice.
Through His redeeming power,
He rose! And we will rise.

If left alone, like some may think,
We'd be unhappy, full of strife.
But we've been taught, with an earnest faith,
We too can have new life!

Our Savior offers help divine
Through His merits, mercy and grace.
He offered Himself a sacrifice for sin
And we shall again behold His face.
How grateful I am for this knowledge from God
It is something I must share.
So that with Christ I may be
Forever with my family there.

Transform

He saved me with His life,
He promises never to stray.
He gives me of His light,
In truth, He is the way.

Why question His sure promises,
Why fear things won't work out?
God gives us peace and comfort,
While Satan makes us doubt.

We each have a purpose,
We each are unique!
Through Christ's redeeming love,
We have no need to retreat.
Instead we charge
To grow and to shine!
To overcome our mortal flaws,
To rise to our divine.

This knowledge can transform us,
It can change our view of life.
Yes, as we follow our Savior
We can receive His light.

Our Savior

The Savior's blood, which was shed for us all
Has power we can't comprehend.
His act of praying, pleading, and crying
Followed by torture, suffering and dying
Proves He is more than our friend.

Our eldest brother, our Savior,
God's beloved Son
Despised and rejected, mocked by all
His face we cruelly did shun.
He had such power, to command the angels,
Yet in humility did teach.
He loves us dearly; "Come unto me"
Was His sincere beseech.

Through His life, His sinless life
He showed us how to act.
By following His pure example
Our joy shall never lack.

He Gives Me Hope

My heart pounds loud, no one can hear.
My heart fills with doubt, no one is near.
My heart's courage wanes, no one is free.
My heart loses hope, no one knows me.

A quiet feeling comes over me,
A quiet whisper says "believe".
A quiet strength begins to seep,
A quiet hope, a needed relief.

His humble life, His path though rough,
His humble act makes ours enough.
His humble bleeding on the tree,
His humble cries of agony.

He radiates life upon the earth,
He radiates love long before His birth.
He radiates comfort on our every fret,
He radiates blessings with every breath.

The Lord walks with us when on our feet.
The Lord cries with us when on our knees.
The Lord guides our path, so we don't go alone.
The Lord wants us back, so He willingly atoned.

My heart pounds loud for I know He can hear.
My heart fills with faith, yes, I know He is near.
My heart's courage grows, through Him I am set free.
My heart gathers hope for my Savior knows me.

This Life

When the creation began,
God had one plan in mind,
That of helping His children
Achieve glorious designs.
So He made this grand world,
Filled with wondrous things,
Even trials and heartaches
He deemed as blessings.

So with creation accomplished,
Smiling down on the Earth
Our Heavenly Father
Awaited your birth.
Having planned the strengths
And weaknesses He'd give
He was excited to see
How you would choose to live.

But knowing that you could not do this alone
And wanting you to see that through trials you had grown,
To Earth He sent His beloved son
Who conquered death, the victory won.
If we will but turn and come unto Him
This life becomes a gift, and joy we will win.
When you see our Father at the end of this journey,
Looking back on this life, smiling not mourning.
When on His right hand you are standing again,
You will see He has become your true constant friend.

You Are Never Alone

He held on to the back of my bike
And said, "this time I'm letting go"
"No!" I shouted, "I can't do this!"
"Don't worry," He says, "you are never alone."
I tug my helmet tighter,
I steadied my trembling knees
"I know that you can do this"
Are His words upon the breeze.

The lights are bright, I feel so scared,
With a gasp my voice cries out.
In my mother's arms, Father smiling at me,
My pounding heart calms down.

Her grin spreads wide as I stand up tall,
Only wobbling once or twice
She says, "come on, come walk to me"
And with hope, I give it a try.

"We love you" they say, thinking I'm asleep
With the blanket pulled over my head.
A warmth spreads across my softening heart,
Maybe they really aren't that bad.

My bags are packed, my mission assigned,
From Dad, a last word of advice.
A hug from Mom then off I go
As tears well up in my eyes.

The camera snaps on our beautiful faces,
Three generations of women.
"She has Dad's eyes," a blessing,
So we can still see him.

"I hate you!" she screams.
"What do I do, how do I help her, please?"
I remember being just like her,
Through Mom's eyes I now see.

The sun is bright, I can't complain,
That's how she would want it to be.
Maybe the brilliant rays of sunlight
Are her way of smiling down on me.

The whirling beeping machine
Giving air to keep me on earth.
This air can take and give life,
The first thing needed at birth.

My family is filled with sadness,
But joy mingles with my tears.
I'm now with my God and my Savior again,
After those brief earthly years.
He says "well done, my daughter,
You served me to the end."
I say "Yes, I remember you!
In life you were my friend.
When in anger I closed you out,
You were there to soften my heart.
You taught me that through obedience,
Thy knowledge you would impart.
Through your loving actions,
You taught me how to serve.
When sorrows and trials came my way,
I served and did not mourn."

He promised at the start
That I would never be alone.
I learned that what He meant
Was He would send Christ to atone.
Whenever I was crying,
Filled with fear and pain,
He reached out in understanding,
Offering His peace again.
When trials were hard,
And feeling happy was harder
He didn't just say, "It'll be fine."
He worked and labored, healing me from within,
Giving me peace overtime.

It was hard to see Him if I wasn't looking.
It was easier to think I was alone.
It made more sense for Him to leave me
Than for Him to stay with someone broken.
But He was there,
He never once left my side.
God promised protection,
And gave Christ to abide.

So, don't think for one minute
That He would leave you comfortless.
God's plan is for our joy
And our eternal happiness.
"I'm thankful for thy promises,
For thy constant guiding hand.
I'm grateful for the life Christ lived,
So that with thee I can live again"

In Our Place

His peaceful smile, a welcome sight,
A lovely reminder from God
This Christ, who walked the very earth
Like us with feet sandal shod,
Relinquished His throne
So that He could atone
For the sins of this mortal sod.

He willingly took upon himself
Our struggles, our sorrow, our pain.
Dignity and honor not being His goal,
He chose instead to remain
With sinners and beggars,
Forsaken lepers.
Joy, He prayed they'd attain.

He paved the way and established the path,
The only way we could go home.
With each added sin He felt the weight increased,
His strength grew with every groan.
He chose to endure it,
The limitless atonement
So that we never must feel alone.

So that smile we see, a divine feature,
That lights up His heavenly face
Reminds us of all He has suffered for,
He's given us infinite grace
We'd be lost and forgotten,
Nothing without Him,
Yes, indeed He stood in our place.

When He Comes Again

Singing His praises,
Shouting His name
Crying Hosanna
That righteous He remains.
Clapping and cheering
Pouring out joyful tears;
Our savior has come again
To calm our fears.

He descends from above
Bringing hope through the clouds.
He offers salvation,
But we mustn't be proud.
When Christ healed the sick
He inquired on their faith.
When in humility they answered
He poured out His grace.
As in days of old
Christ still offers us healing.
The promise of strength
Through our faith is His blessing.

We follow His path,
We walk His way,
We keep the commandments
And improve every day.
He lifts us up to live
With our father above.
This life we have is a gift
Given from Heaven, in love.

He offers life eternal
And helps us endure to the end.
Through His atoning sacrifice
Our broken hearts, He mends.
So, when I see His face
Smiling down from the sky
I trust Him and His healing grace,
That He will lift me high.

I'm on His Side

The pain that engulfed me
Fails to compare;
The Joy of my Savior
Overcomes my despair.
He offers life eternal
Filling my soul with relief.
The price of this gift
Is only to believe.

I have seen Him heal
The most broken of hearts.
I have felt Him lift me
When I fall apart.
I have heard, and attested,
That just the use of His name
Can cast away darkness
Bringing forth light and new day.
In me, if I have faith,
He will work miracles.
With His strength buoying me up,
Nothing is impossible.

Does He claim He has power
Only some of the time?
Does He promise to walk with us
And then stray from our side?
While the world all around us
Operates on 'what if',
Christ's promises are sure,
And He says we are His.
While others may vacillate
And follow Satan's lies,
I know of Christ's love.
I'm on His side.

We Are Meant to Grow

We strive to do our Father's will,
To show Him that we care.
To prove that His Son's sacrifice
We always will remember
Sometimes we find that we are weak,
We lack strength on our own.
But then our Father's loving son
Promised us He would atone.

This life is filled with ups and downs,
Often trials will come our way.
If we but choose to follow Him
He will never lead us astray.

In our Father's eyes we are so young,
There's but little that we know
And so He gives many tools to us
That from our trials we may grow.
If the path we walk is straight uphill
There is no need to fear.
Through trying, failing, repenting, and changing
To our Savior, we will draw near.

Strength of Christ

When seeing us stumbling
Seeing us fall
Our simple faith waning
We begin to withdraw.
Our courage has faltered,
Our strength is shot,
But to lie here, beaten,
Was not why Christ fought
With the weight of our sins,
Fought with the pains of our life,
With our heartaches,
With our sorrows and strife.
He fought these, triumphant!
He'd fight them again.
Through knowing our pains
He can now succor them.

So, He walks with us daily,
Our pillar of strength.
He offers compassion
So that we may at length
See Him beside us,
Holding our hands,
Realize that always
He was our constant friend.
We look there behind us,
Our life laid out plain.
He was our strength
Again and again.

He directed our course,
Put up guardrails and signs;
He pointed us home
Then stayed by our side.
He kept us from straying,
Intent on our success.
Even trials and heartaches
He knew would be best.
When we realize His efforts,
His help we finally see,
In awe and gratitude
We fall to our knees.
We praise Him and thank Him,
He pulls us up from the earth.
He smiles and says
"Nothing exceeds your worth."

Be Still

How many times does our dear Father's love

Fall

Upon closed hardened ears?
How many times does He offer us help but we

Too prideful

Won't hear.
How many times must He say "You're enough" without our retort

"But I'm not?"

How long will it take us truly to trust Him, honestly, with nothing held back, open our hearts and make vulnerable our walls, see Him, follow Him, love ourselves as He does, and finally, finally

Believe Him!

He knows the way, even He made the path
He felt our pains before our first cry.
That when we find weakness, our built-up strength failing
we never need
more than to try.
His arm shoots out toward us the moment we falter
while we signal
"no!"

or "please heal!"

If we will but let Him and fight Him no more,
then His strength becomes so real.
He is ready and waiting while our storm is still raging
He offers us peace through the words
"Be still."

I'm Enough

So, what if I'm not perfect now?
Do I need to be today?
Does it make my worth any less?
I'm still following His way.

So, what if I'm not humble yet?
Does it mean I'm filled with pride?
Christ knows I am doing my best
For He sees what's inside.

So, what if I know all He asks,
Yet while trying I still fail?
Was His suffering and dying on the cross
Useless, or to no avail?

He labored in the garden,
He labored up the hill,
He has labored on the cross,
His labor of love was God's will.

Our Savior went through pain and grief,
He died in agony.
Thus, feeling all my sins and sorrows,
He offers forgiveness to me!

He knew that our perfection,
Was not too easily won.
To save us from pain and misery,
He became the one
Who bore our burdens,
Lifted us up
From each of our lips,
He took our bitter cup.

So, what if I am caring
And treat others with love?
My will is what Christ asks for;
When I give that, I'm enough.

He Loves Completely

I seek for His guidance
I pray for His care.
I know He is listening
I know He's aware.

He smiles down lovingly
Each time I reach out
With joy in my asking
He gives blessings of help.

He is my Brother
He loves me so
He is my redemption
He's all I need and more.

He is my Savior
He is my friend.
He is my Salvation
And I shall live again.

I try so hard
To show Him I will stay true
To say to Him in actions
"I'll always trust in you"

He is my Lord
He is all I need
He hears every prayer
He hears every plea

He is strong and mighty
While I'm weak and small
Yet He loves me so deeply
He loves us all.

And so, while I fail
And while I still fall
He loves me completely
He died for me after all.

After all I can do
While I'm still trying hard
To show Him my will
His love and strength imparts.
He doesn't need perfection
He doesn't need my strength
He doesn't need much of anything
He blesses me at length.

The only thing that I can give
The only thing that is my own
I'll give to Him my simple will
The way that He has shown.

He Chose Us

He paid for all our sins and pains
This gift was high in price.
Though meriting nothing of ourselves
He willingly sacrificed
His perfect, sinless, healing life
For sinners, you and me.
That then through His atoning love
Perfected we may be.

Try as we may to reach Heaven alone,
We simply cannot attain
The blessings of Heaven, come from our Savior's love
His forgiveness we must always retain.
His arms stretched out wide,
His smile still wider
He beckons us. "Come unto me."
His words offer peace, a release in my soul
The blessings of sweetest relief.

We Choose Him

Don't say no to discipleship,
Don't say no to Christ.
Don't say no to shining
Christ's glorious light.
When Christ the master shepherd
Commanded, "Feed my sheep"
This Christ the master teacher
Commanded us to teach.

A testimony of Christ's life
Directly comes from living
The gospel truths He died for
Our example is one way of giving
Our life to show we follow Him
This witness that we give
Helps others feel eternal love
From Christ who truly lives.

Believe

In seeing all our weaknesses,
In knowing all we lack,
How do we recognize God's love
Not as fiction, but as fact?
In finding we are nothing,
How do we discover our worth?
How do we see God's grand design
For us here on the earth?

The plan was laid out long before
He made His mortal journey.
He knew the price He'd have to pay
To rescue you and me.
He knew that He would be esteemed
As not much above the dust.
He knew they'd curse and swear His name
After He died there for us.

Yet in His infinite wisdom,
And knowing all His pain,
He chose to follow God's will
And sent His will away.
With every breath that He took in
His body was racked with anguish for us.
He gives another saving breath,
To plead for our forgiveness.

If we indeed mean nothing,
Then why would our Savior die?
Why would He teach and heal us,
If in the grand scheme, we would just pass by?
He tells us that He loves us,
He knows our every need.
Blessings He has in store for us.
We must, in turn, believe.

The Best Gift

How great is the pain
He must endure;
Watching us in our pride,
Knowing how we will suffer.
He wants us to return,
He wants us home and safe.
He wants us to follow Him
And avoid the path of strife.

If we refuse
His outstretched hand,
What more can He do?
But He never stops
Reaching out to us.
Our strength He hopes to renew.

So, while we battle
With grief and pain
We must strive to never forget
That if we grasp
His pleading hand,
Our life He is sure to bless.

With humility, now
Our newest strength,
Bought through our repentance,
Our constant friend,
Even Christ the Lord,
Offers us the best gifts.

Saving Grace

In pleading with the Father, petitioning the Son
I strive to pray with real intent.
I tell my Father all my cares, my worries, and my sorrows.
I do my best to repent.
I know the Savior felt my pains and try to remember this truth.
I feel His power to erase,
He says through faith I have been made whole!
This is truly saving grace.

He Draws Near unto Me

I cannot see Him, cannot hear Him,
Cannot prove He's there,
Yet through a happy, peaceful feeling
I know that He's aware.
He has my life completely planned,
All part of His design
And when I give my will to Him
I see it's greater than mine.

That's all I have to give, my will,
He has claim to all else,
So when I say, "Thy will, not mine,"
Then this is what He tells:

"You are my beloved child,
You're worth more than you know.
Please let me take the reins, and see!
We'll conquer every foe.
You cannot go through life alone,
That's why I gave my son,
To suffer, bleed, and die for you,
Even if you were the only one."

Even if He only saved one soul,
One brother or sister of His,
He would suffer, bleed, and die for me,
To be able to return and live.
The love I see in that sacred act
Is more than I comprehend,
He gave His perfect life, for me,
To someday be with God again.

With hope made bright through His sinless life,
I have no need to fear.
For through His birth, His life, His death,
I always have Him near.
With trust and love within my heart,
I finally can see
That when I draw near unto Him,
He draws near unto me.

Will I Be There

On days when the sun shines warmly through the leaves
When the sweet smell of nature lingers on the air
I can almost sense the wisdom of the trees
They stood alert when the Savior was there.

But for Him that long night was a harsh end to the day
He went to the garden to accomplish the impossible.
Calling out to His Father as His strength began to sway
Yet He was the only one who was able.

He gave up His life, not at all a small task
He loved us enough to suffer our pains
He followed the Father and did exactly as was asked
The onlookers in ignorance viewed with disdain

But the trees stood there stalwart not leaving His side
Not drifting off into helpless sleep
Their unfailing strength gives us a guide
How to endure, for the blessings to reap.

Like the trees in the garden who spent time with their master
Can we watch with them just the same?
Can we prove as disciples that to His course we are sure?
On our hearts, have we written His name.

Act in Faith

As I seek to see thy loving hand,
As I pray to know thy will,
As I search the words you've given me
I strive in my life to fulfill
All the plans that you have made for me,
All the joy you have in store.
All the knowledge that you will impart
If I will just implore!

Persistent efforts, acted in faith,
Doing all we've been commanded,
Will lead to joy and great delight,
In receiving these promised blessings.
Sometimes our Savior needs to see
Our faith before He gives
The strength to live and do His will,
Then do His will and live.

He Teaches Grace

As His witness,
His disciple,
His follower;
I want to show my faith.
As my brother,
My Savior,
The Son of God,
He wants to teach us grace.

As a child,
I'm lacking wisdom.
As a mortal,
I'm not perfect.
As the Savior,
He says regardless
Of my flaw,
His light I can reflect.

At first
My thoughts are callous,
My deeds
Not more than reactions.
But as He teaches
The art of grace
My life fills up
With passion!

When I see the need of another,
I rush to bring them aid,
To help them bear their burdens,
As the Savior does each day.

As His converted follower,
I want to live in His light.
As His trusted disciple,
I want to choose the right.
I want to mourn with those in mourning,
Give comfort to the comfortless.
To stand up tall as a witness of God
And of His transcendent grace.

His Peace

I'm struggling to hear Him
As this intense fear descends.
Satan turns my faith against me
Using doubt as His weapon.
The waves of panic, looming overhead
Threaten upon me to crash.
Again, I loosen my grip on faith;
Though needing help, I forgot to ask.
Spiraling downward in panic and terror
The light above seems to dim.
Maybe this was how I had to learn
I need only rely on Him.

Like the calm that follows a raging storm
Christ stills the tumultuous waters.
Stretching out His mighty hand,
Peace is what He offers.
I reach for His hand
Which He grasps with affection.
With feelings of shame,
I await His rejection.

I had ignored His sound counsel,
On wrong paths, I had strayed.
Shouldn't He leave me also?
I had not followed His way.

Knowing my thoughts
And hearing my heart,
He accepts my repentance,
Forgiveness He imparts.
He is filled with power
And love is His name;
With my sins now forgiven
My soul He will not defame.
He instead pours out peace,
A healing salve made from grace.
With my doubts now behind me
I move forward in faith.

Choose Happiness

Choose happiness.
Choose Christ.
Choose joy.
Throughout your life.

Make the change,
Wherever you are.
Choosing to smile
Will help you go far.

Christ who is perfect
Gave us the truth,
If we follow His ways,
Joy is our fruit.

So, choose to smile.
Choose to shine.
Be an example
Of God's love, divine.

Trust

To give up hope because we cannot
See the path ahead
Is to say and accept that, without knowing, we cannot
Be led.
To give into temptation and to relent our faith to
Doubt
Is to feed the adversary, our heart with emptiness
Resounds.
To sit down in the sand and to give up
On our course
Is to forfeit our trust in God and stop
Relying on the Lord.

Trusting in God and
Relying on the Lord
Is to rise up from the sand and continue
On our course.
Denying the adversary and letting the strength in my heart
Resound
Is to resist temptation and, with faith, overcome
Doubt.
To believe, without knowing, that we indeed can
Be led.
Is to grasp our hope and move forward as though we
See the path ahead.

Grace

Don't try to hide
Your tears
Don't try to act like you
Don't fear
The only way
He can lift us up
Is if we let go
And give Him our trust
When you fall
To your knees,
When you feel
You can hardly breathe,
When your fears
Overcome your faith,
You can trust,
You can trust in grace.

He's calling your name
He's crying out
He wants nothing more
No nothing more
Than to lift you up
Then to hold you tight
To give you strength
To watch you take flight.

So now we'll
Dry our tears
And He will help
Us rid our fears.
The only way
He can lift us up
Is if we let go
And give Him our trust.
When you rise
From your knees,
When you feel
You can hardly breathe,
When your fears
Are overcome by faith,
You can trust,
You can trust in grace.

To Trust Is to Live

Please bless us, dear Father,
Lift us up on eagle wings.
Knowing joy soon will come
Gives us strength to begin.
With the path laid out plain, and
Only details are obscured,
The main rule we have
Is to trust in the Lord.

Beginning our journey,
We ask too many questions,
Wanting an answer to every "what if."
Wasting time with our worries
We lose sight of our blessings,
And forget that to trust is to live.

So, Christ shows us one step,
Only one at a time;
The way He also learned,
Line upon line.
More substantial than breadcrumbs
He leaves a trail of hope.
The goal sweeter than a candy house,
Eternal life is what He shows.

When the trial seems too big,
The elephant more than we can eat,
Not seeing the final picture,
Our courage wants to retreat.
If we look up above
For the next step to take,
Then look forward and move,
Acting only on faith.
We will find that the path
Is all of God's make
And the trials and blessings
Help make us great.

Though little I know of the way ahead
I take each step with a smile.
For if I trust His perfect path,
I'll see blessings along the miles.

In My Life

I know in my heart
I believe in my mind
My Savior is good
His judgments are kind

I trust in His ways
And seek for His counsel
I pray for strength
To follow His will

I walk in His footsteps
I stay on the path
That leads to salvation
To joy without lack

For I know in my heart
I believe in my mind
That my Savior is good
His judgments are kind.

I know that His plan
For me is the best
Far better than mine
So, I won't protest
To all that He gives me
In joy or in pain
The trials are blessings
This knowledge I've gained
Through trusting
Through faith
Through hope
And through grace

I've looked back on my life
With a view through God's eyes
I've had anger dissolve
My pain melts away
My gratitude swells
He was always there
In my life.

Rise

A feeling of strength
Quite unlike before
Comes over me,
Brings me up from the floor.
My Savior beside me,
His face, all I see.
Was He ever not there
Watching over me?

Never, oh never
Would He ever abandon.
His love is to strong
To leave us on our own.
Nay, He loves us too deeply
To see us feeling low
And not offer us help,
While the answers He knows.

So He lifts us up high,
Plants us right on our feet
While watching afar
He never retreats.
With the waves crashing fiercely,
The storm threatening to overcome,
Drawing near is our Savior,
The risen, Holy one.

He lifts up our burdens
Once we lay them down.
He lifts weary hands,
He will not let us drown.
He lifts failing hearts
Bidding us to feel His scars.
He lifts downcast eyes,
Sets our sights toward the stars.

About the Author

Katerina Lucic Sanders—she's a poet, a musician, and a follower of Christ. She served as a missionary for the Church of Jesus Christ of Latter-Day Saints where her testimony and faith grew exponentially. Seeing the hand of God in her life led Katerina to write poetry, the only expression that seemed to illustrate the feelings that resonated inside. As words began to flow into her mind, she started piecing together rhymes and stanzas to create *Reflections on the Savior*, her debut book of poetry. Katerina is from the Washington DC area and is currently continuing her education in Utah.

CPSIA information can be obtained
at www.ICGtesting.com
Printed in the USA
FSOW01n0941021117
40474FS